Slower

ANDREW MCNEILLIE is the Literature Editor at Oxford University Press. He was born at Hen Golwyn, Clwyd, in North Wales, and educated at John Bright Grammar School, Llandudno, and at Magdalen College, Oxford. He recently founded Clutag Press, publishing poetry and memoir. His prose memoir *An Aran Keening*, to which several allusions are made in this volume, was published by the Lilliput Press, Dublin, in 2001.

ANDREW McNEILLIE

Slower

CARCANET

First published in Great Britain in 2006 by
Carcanet Press Limited
Alliance House
Cross Street
Manchester M2 7AQ

A CIP catalogue record for this book is available from the British Library
ISBN 1 85754 828 0
978 1 85754 828 0

The publisher acknowledges financial assistance from Arts Council England

Typeset by XL Publishing Services, Tiverton
Printed and bound in England by SRP Ltd, Exeter

for Anna-Mae

Acknowledgements

My first debt of gratitude is to Kyffin Williams for allowing me to use a detail of his seascape *Waves Breaking Over Reef, Trearddur* (1994, oil on canvas) on the cover of this book. (I celebrate him warmly as he knows in 'Glyn Dŵr Sonnets' (no. xiii) and offer him a prayer in poem xi of 'Homage to Patagonia'.) Thanks also to Nicholas Sinclair for facilitating this, and to Adrian Lack. Next I am deeply indebted to Julian Bell for his 'Artwork' to the poem 'Arkwork' and to Michael Schmidt for enthusiastically agreeing to include it *en face* with the poems here. A limited edition of *Arkwork with Artwork* was published by the Clutag Press in March 2006.

Those friends and relations who have encouraged me in the making of these poems know well who they are and why I do not need to name them publicly. Some of the poems here have been previously published in periodicals and I would like to thank the editors of the following for their kindness to me: *Metre, New Welsh Review, Oxford Magazine, Oxford Poetry, PNR* (including 'Arkwork' in its entirety), *Poetry Review, Poetry Wales, Stand* (the sonnet sequence 'Portrait of the Poet as a Young Dog'), *Times Literary Supplement.* 'In Memoriam Edward Thomas (1878–1917)' was commissioned for a volume forthcoming from Enitharmon to celebrate Thomas's life and work; 'In Memoriam Carey Morris RA (1882–1968)' will also appear in that collection.

Contents

quick progress day by day, and slower
week by week, a task, as the proverb
says like fetching water over a river.

GLYN DŴR SONNETS (xxiv)

Cotsplut! there's bastards for you.

DAVID JONES, *In Parenthesis*

For any sake... could you not hold less noise!

MARY McNEILLIE

Honeysuckle

I bought a trellis to support a vine.
The vine was slow to wind itself
out of the earth and climb.
For several seasons I wondered where
responsibility lay, whether with myself
and want of patience or
poor stock or soil or something on the air.

So I would look from my window
of an idle hour, waiting,
like a prisoner staring out through
his solitary confinement's little grating,
at the course of time.
And the vine still scarcely grew
as if daunted by that trellis frame.

So things went until I took
no care in it, troubling neither to
pluck it out nor study honeysuckle in a book.
And so it grew, and slowly grew
time out of mind and now
trellis and vine embrace, as if,
for all the world, for dear life.

Stones

The stones on my sill hold their cold
ovals and angles steadily, rock steady.
Lodestones to my uprootedness they
anchor me, weigh me up and down, all told,
though I leave out of mind the place
I took them from, for charm and talisman,
for that burden's too full a refrain
ever to be my saving grace.

Mornings I cover them with outspread
hands and feel them numb to the bone,
as if I reached for them in a streambed.
They're as cold, god knows, as ice,
like the gaze of one who has
the measure of you and all you ever said.

In Memoriam Vernon Watkins (1906–1967)

I published a poem in America,
in *Shenandoah*, courtesy of Greer
& Dabney. Of which I remember
nothing, neither title nor idea,
but the image of a magpie ladling light
and dark. I stole *Poetry for Supper*
by R. S. Thomas (the higher hunger)
from a Swansea bookshop, black and white
indeed. Thieving magpie on £5 a week
and penny-a-line. You think I joke? I
sent poems to Vernon Watkins who wrote back
that he never described for its own sake.
Truth's metaphysical beyond the eye.
Then he died. What did he mean, for god's sake?

Older than we are by however many ages,
it doesn't need defending against anything.
(Far more do air and fire, earth and water.)
Not even in our empty times. Neglected, it will
go underground, or into interstellar space.

Until out of nowhere someone calls it up,
like the Greek who cut my hair last week.
Where was he from? 'Spar-ta,' he said.
'You are a Spartan!' I exclaimed. 'Oh no,'
he said, 'there are no Spartans anymore.'

The State of Play on the Rialto

These days he haunts me everywhere I go
as even on a mid-life week in Venice,
washed up at the Guggenheim, I notice
La Nostalgie du poète by de Chirico.
It turns me on like the blue note at the bridge
across the Amman, the blind stare's in-
stress inscrutable, as fish or mannequin,
a life lived always elsewhere on the edge.

How could Orpheus with his song and lyre
not look back and quit the race while still ahead
or face the music of his heart's desire?
Not the thing-in-itself but the other
thing-in-itself, haunting shade, alienated,
that is poetry's eternal power?

Thirty-Six Exposures

for Robert Macfarlane

A shadow-boxing hare.
A fine spring evening.
The blackbird's shutter-speed gape.
A human embryo in its twelfth week.
Face to face with William Blake.
The gannet's stoop.
The revelation at Belsen.
The poet's rolling eye.
The bloom of youth.
A night out in Chernobyl.
Firstlight on the 1st of March.
A curlew cry.
A wedding party.
A new brood.
A new broom.
The tyrant before the firing squad.
Hugh MacDiarmid sober.
A goldfinch in a thistle cloud.
The Easter Rising.
Not the eleventh but the last of September.
Swallows staving off departure.
The dying stare.
A snake in Ireland.
The 5th of November.
Shakespeare's juvenilia.
An ordered garden.
My funeral procession.
Kyffin making waves at Trearddur.
North Clutag kitchen in midwinter.
Fighting in the streets.
The language map of Wales in 3000.
The last English speaker on earth (*aetat* 103).
That first trout in the smithy burn.
A Bloody Butcher, a Coch-y-bonddu.
Ae fond kiss
and then another.
The dark backward and abysm of time.

To a Critic

'Our age prefers a light touch…'
Someone's acquired a plural,
someone's acquired an age.
If it isn't too much trouble
may time prove his scourge.

Portrait of the Poet as a Young Dog

for Diana Maureen Porter

(i) Diana and Actaeon

This is the subject beyond all others
that once again will turn me upside
down: so Actaeon had no place to hide
and no defence, for all his antlers.
I steel myself to failure just the same
as I did when youthful lust propelled me,
longing for you, whoever you might be,
before I even knew your name.

This is the story that's as old as time
or young as it and writes itself
according to the formulae: sublime
and ridiculous, at once. However
it turns out, happily, or comes to grief,
it is of all of them, forever after.

(ii) Hume's Enquiry

Just as I might believe I've signalled my
intention here, so with a longing look
and then another, I turned back from my book
to stare at her, thinking I'd caught her eye,
across the lecture theatre. Hume's *Enquiry*
had no chance against the cause
-and-effect impact of her on my gaze,
and nothing dreamt in his philosophy.

My true Penelope (as the poet said)
wasn't Petrarch's Laura but Zhivago's
Julie Christie, and all the girls from head
to foot her lookalikes in maxi-coats, high boots
(I tell it like it was) and back-combed hairdos.
And all the mophead boys were poets?

10

(iii) *For the Fallen*

for John Barnard

Or so they fancied, in their innocence,
in nineteen-sixty-five and -six. But then
'innocence is no earthly weapon',
and they were nothing of the sort. So tense,
lugubrious Geoffrey Hill, reliably
informed them, in the course of lectures on
poetry from Yeats to Hughes and Gunn,
sweating in his funeral suit of charcoal grey.

His black shirt, in that artificial light,
caught tenebrous hues, green as Baudelaire
's dyed hair; his pudgy face so queer,
his brow so damp, as if he spent the night
in hell-on-earth, every day of the year,
and knew he was the only poet there.

(iv) Esse est percipi

He was for me at least the only show
in town (Christ, what a pantomime!), except
for Quentin Bell, whose teasing humour kept
'bad art' in the picture, and taught me how
deeply gravity may depend on laughter,
and vice versa. Thoughts on De Gustibus
(tasteless! tasteless!) still make me focus…
on how we cannot read the future.

But it was in philosophy
I could count on the thought that I'd see her.
Esse est percipi opined Berkeley.
Oh don't tell me what I know already:
to be is to be perceived, but would she ever,
or would she never, perceive me?

(v) *A Vision of Reality*

The youth from Wales as silent as the hills,
shore-dweller, mountain-haunter, 's truly
an innocent abroad, however guilty,
lost in that world, for want of social skills.
He dreams and drowns in so much liberty:
Tetley's, John Smith's, Magnet Ales,
the like of which were never sunk in Wales,
or not while gazing on A VISION OF REALITY.

Not her but 'A Study of Liberalism in
Twentieth-century Verse' by Frederick Grubb,
a sort of Lives of the Poets, open
in his lap at Yeats, Eliot, Auden…
Thomas, his worm's eye fiddle and hubbub,
thrown in as if to bring me down.

(vi) L'Albatros

It is no sin to lose your way, whatever
price the gods exact, backwoods boy in
the urban night, homesick, courting ruin,
through a glass darkly. Hell or high water,
see him cross the street like an albatross
to catch the last bus back to Lawnswood,
as if he weirdly understood
the path to truth begins in loss.

How else might the heart ever know beauty?
As just a bourgeois entertainment,
good taste converted into booty?
But forget all that… Whenever will he
get to meet her? So between sonnet
and sonnet here, even I begin to worry.

(vii) *Like a Rolling Stone*

On the day he'd betray the girl from home,
he drove with the boys over Ilkley Moor,
in a black Ford Pilot, out looking for
'The Twelve Apostles', singing as they came:
'Hey! You! Get off of my cloud…' Driving
around, from cloud to cloud they sped
up-hill-down-dale until the sky bled
and night closed in about their skiving.

Repairing to the Skyrack and the skite,
he slipped out unobserved, undercover,
awol from the crowd to keep his date.
O dear woman, whatever were you thinking,
as I stole up to be your lover
in best clandestine style for kissing?

(viii) *i.m.* Le Deuxième Sexe

I can still remember the instant when
I sensed her scent, the touch of her,
taste of her mouth, her aura… O daughter
of de Beauvoir… what passion drove you then?
First, never second, sex, you second-guessed
my gaze and asked me nothing in return
but what you gave was all I had to learn
however long it took that we were blessed.

The signs we read or else read us may be
signs of our times that time alone translates.
I see our like now and invisibly pass by,
on the other side. In vain to tell them
their icons are as dust before the Fates,
all hormones and biology the dream?

(ix) 'The Tree' Revisited

But once we've dreamt it, how we can't
help but mourn it? Midnight had them
canoodling in the Hollies, *carpe noctem*:
Zhivago's Russia had no colder brunt
than that northern winter's starry wind
like a sharp blast blown from Siberia.
So he played Yury to her Lara
and never thought how things might end.

The poems he wrote for her told where
he came from (courtesy of Thomas & Co)
but none the less failed to dissuade her.
As did 'The Tree' which, so he said,
betrays no strength but as the winds blow,
gives, and bides its time, and keeps its head.

(x) *Northern House*

As she at least did. I couldn't say
the same for him, with his sudden antlers
wired-up out through the branching stars,
over the hills and far away
in Wales. There Christmas laboured and,
conscienceless, he relished with delight
the double life; and lay awake at night,
longing for her, with his pen to hand.

O juvenilia! Still they said they'd
do a pamphlet. Somewhere I have proof,
up there, north-north-west, inside my head.
That box of vanities beneath the roof,
the place most poems meet their end.
For which give thanks, imaginary friend.

(xi) *In Vaucluse*

for John Fuller

So late, so soon, the crisis came and time
to pack his bags and books and sling his hook,
a statistic in the failure rate. His look
a fallen angel's. Disgrace and shame
at home heaped on him for his wild folly.
So off he set intent upon his quest
and journeyed to the bottom of the worst,
heart-wounded in Vaucluse, just north of Swansea.

But you know already my dog's leg story.
To those who don't it's hardly gripping news.
What is the end of autobiography?
This ruse to simulate a date with fate,
to try again to best the muse
at some point of no return: so soon, so late?

We are having the worst of weather
but the days are getting longer and
we've had enough of the short ones…
I wake and while the kettle boils peer out
into the gloom, thinking of your letter.

Ashore here inkwash daybreak floods
sooner than it did the day before,
and the equinoctial laurel lunges,
the hawthorn shakes forked lightning
out of earth's cracked egg.

Death

How many times was it those foggy anaesthetic days
when I could hardly see a hand before my eyes but felt your breath?
I've learnt not to look for an intelligent answer from you...
But I remember that break-of-day you stood your ground for once,
as if it was yesterday, and I travelling the low road of my idyll,
knowing this was it at last and he was with you.
Nothing I thought or said could alter that. He'd not stir
if I slipped my hand under the blanket and shook his foot
the way he used to do to me, afraid we might be late
for the morning rise and shine up there in Paradise.

How many times but never again like that, not now I know you
for what you are? Like the back of my hand, as they say,
your grip tightening even as it loses hold, has lost its hold
on reason, now on life, as you loiter there as if to be sure this is it.
And what then is it after all but nothing we knew wouldn't happen?
Still I sat on there watching those signs of nothing gather,
as if incredulous. It haunted me for weeks of mourning
I can tell you, dumbly, down all my failure
to love anyone adequately, inadequate to know my feelings
and to make them known. As now I see too late.

This is how I search my wounds:
feeling my pockets from outside.

Patting them to check, for example,
spectacles and verses are to hand.

Gone for Good

How many more poems will you haunt,
old man? I know you won't say, but
don't pretend you're not keeping count.
I know you and I know you're not done yet.
As on those endless dour days you'd cast
and cast into the evening and keep casting
while I'd pray the next would be your last
not knowing then that faith is everlasting.

My mother said you just upped and left
but that was ever your way, if you could.
Given half a chance to fish I'd do the same.
There's nothing new except we are bereft
and now we say you've gone for good
which so far hasn't lived up to its name.

I must be bananas or bird-brained myself
drifting at the margins of this moorland lake
to be so taken by the sight of it, even if it is
a rare one here, a lost soul, calling like a siren to me.
Seen once it calls to my eye to discover it again,
but I can't in the wind-drift waftage where
the water beats and saps at a stand of conifer
and even the stones and pebbles seem yellow.

Something in the light and chopping water
keeps it from me. I'm far out, anyway, in a
trance-state, fishing all day for reluctant trout.
My boat yields to the waves, rolling, my rod
to casting. Nothing else yields, but I yield
to *tsweep* and *tsweep* and sweep my oars and stare at sound,
flicking my line out to and fro. The bird,
for all it calls out, to and fro, might not be there.

What might be? *Tsweep...* spirit. I remember how
they thought I had a short attention span but I had
the longest there is, and it still holds good refuge now
from common or garden grief. The rod I wield
bears my father's name, and in his hand,
varnished over. I fished this water with him.
The world is not simply a place of privileged effects
or hindsight could be truly twenty-twenty.

Yet I can look now and see him intimately.
If heart is not sure, what can be? It's feelings I look for
and into, in every sense, and nothing called escape
but respite only. The bleached firs wrecked
at the water's edge, he told me, are skeletons
of giant fish, picked clean by a bear the size of Ursa Major,
and all shooting stars are yellow wagtails.
And make of it what you will I believed him.

The Fisher Widow

'No angler is ever complete…
… not even in death.'
So he said to me laughing
at the very thought of what he'd said
and set me thinking how
the best ones are the ones
that get away, as he has done.
Who better than he to know?

Plato hooked a paradigm, all right,
if not to everybody's liking
or for all seasons, in and out.
I have a healthy appetite.
I do prefer to eat my trout.
But up there where the granite air
chastens light and water
the idea itself can be enough.

Among the gifts he gave his bride
was an illustrated Walton.
She never dabbled otherwise
but grew to be grateful for
her fisher-widow's compensation:
to have the house to herself
when he was on the mountain.
Though now she tells another story.

An end does not produce further result,
said Aristotle. Whatever he meant
about beginnings and middles and ends
he surely knew it does. Only consult
your heart, and how it has been rent,
to feel the aftershocks increase, as friends
exit – the direction reads *exeunt*
omnes... – backstage, where the action's felt.

And that itself might be an end to it,
for grief's a frugal school. It teaches how
to make ends meet, and that you must move on.
So you must, and call it a day. But call it
what you will, and put it behind you now,
the song's not over though the singer's gone.

Hedge Fund

How they clutch at my heart,
last year's birds' nests
in the mind's bare branches
this New Year's Day.
Stuff in manuscript,
ink-squiggle and thicket.

How long will it weather?
Will it see spring?
With what hope or luck,
refurbishment, revision,
rethreading tweak of the pen
clutch your heart as well?

In the clutter of his studio
he made what I took to be trench tea,
leaves in the cup, hot water. No, Tommy
knew no such luxury, oh no…
But those leaves about my gums and teeth
made me gag as if a whiff of gas still
lingered on the air he breathed, enough to kill
a green recruit like me, or hasten death.

But death spared him then. He was a fighter,
this South Wales Borderer of the Slade
and Newlyn schools, a wheezy raconteur,
who told how Edward Thomas would call by,
sit where I sat, with that 'doomed look' he had,
as if already claimed for history.

Meditation on Armistice Day

in memoriam Corporal Joe Hoyles MM, no. 3697, 13th Rifle Brigade, B Company

I'll step in here where barely legible advice
to trespassers lies in the ditch, fungus
chewing a corner of it, as if it's starving.
But there's so much to devour here in this
rackety winter wood... I nearly wrote mood,
you'd lose your mind trying to account for it.

The burnt-out house by now almost
metamorphosed into ash-trees, ashes to ashes,
haunting here like Colonel Johnny's ghost.
So I imagine. The mind has forests of them
and true stories that wind through them
like that little burn I once stole along half-scared.

How a place can be a shadow of its former self,
in process of forgetting here. Even the non-biodegradables
that skirt the hedge, the trash of trash, take on
a bloom of dirt and algae, the life of atoms,
microscopic winter spores, clues to death
by a thousand myopic cuts, oozing all away.

The only way out is not through but round?
Like the chainsaw blade and the blue whiff
of two-stroke and resinous dust, to dust. If it were
as easy to tend the mind, with its dead wood
and undergrowth fermenting and fomenting,
I would join the Forestry Commission's ambulance brigade.

Meanwhile, uncle, the day bends to its task, convex, concave,
it billows light and beats its bounds with
bare branches like lackeys of some old estate
for towering pheasants where beeches make
a stand and in the hollow the guns volley
as far back as Mametz Wood, where the Welsh went at it.

Glyn Dŵr Sonnets

The race that is oppressed shall prevail in the end,
for it will resist the savagery of the invaders.

from 'The Prophecies' of Merlin

(i)

So he retreated… into history, his life
no better documented than the Bard's.
That nation-building chronicler of strife
who taught the Welsh the harm in English words.
'Glendower' might just suspend our disbelief
but at central casting, for all eternity,
in Hollywood and Hell (if not in Glyndyfrdwy),
Fluellen rules, and *Taffy was a thief…*

I imagine, after the recent raids, after
the carpet bombing and interrogation
at Camp X-Ray, how they gathered together
at news-time, to see S4C's latest
relay from an obscure Breton station:
the sound of his voice; and then the forecast.

(ii)

At Pumlumon expect foul weather…
When it's summer elsewhere, it's winter in
Wales, the saying goes. But what a summer
they enjoyed, the white settlers of Llŷn.
Oh when it's summer in Wales, it's winter
in the soul's bare hearth, is what they mean:
as if the rain cried its eyes out forever,
to wash away their failure like a stain.

I think particularly of that damp squib
Lewis Valentine and his cronies lit
at Penyberth and served nine months for.
'They forgot the matches,' was the glib
local jest… And so to the victor
the spoils, and to the vanquished, wit.

26

(iii) *'Mr De Valera's Hint to the English in Wales'*

'It is possible…' De Valera said,
addressing a thousand teachers at Caernarfon,
in nineteen-fifty, not urging a re-run
with fireworks at the Post Office and dead
in the streets come Easter to Caerdydd,
but out from Dublin simply to explain…
'…to lose your freedom and win it back again.
But lose your language and *Cymru am byth*
can never be but Wales forever lost.'
(I interpret the gist.) Ireland looked to
the Welsh example. Ireland knew the cost.
English should be taught as a second language.
And I'm thinking now I'd like to know
what the Home Office made of his homage.

(iv)

Soon after, seething with *ressentiment*
(ever to have been born outside Scotland),
I'd blush to my roots to understand
what the mutation of consonants meant,
stumbling like a dunce where native sons
excelled, for a handful of hours a week,
the tables briefly turned. My lot to speak
'the Queen's English' (let bygones be bygones?),

if not my common fantasy or dream
which mostly ran on marbles, or penknives,
or hooks to catch a trout in Colwyn stream.
While my ear tuned itself to the music in
Cymraeg in English and our daily lives,
our inscapes, aspiring to *cynefin*.

(v) Cynefin *Glossed*

What is another language? Not just words
and rules you don't know, but concepts too
for feelings and ideas you never knew,
or thought, to name; like a poem that floods
its lines with light, as in the fabled
origin of life, escaping paraphrase.
So living in that country always was
mysterious and never to be equalled.

For example, tell me in a word how
you'd express a sense of being that
embraces belonging here and now,
in the landscape of your birth and death,
its light and air, and past, at once, and what
cause you might have to give it breath?

(vi) *Owain's Poetics*

The art is to leave your calling card and
melt away. To keep them wondering what
it is you're up to, haunting the page at
the edge of sense, as if you understand
their dreams. Nature's not the only thing that
can't abide a vacuum, myth also
fills in absence, to make a legend grow.
The past might serve to your advantage but
leave prophecy to Merlin (via Hopcyn…)
And the rest is not silence but history.
Meanwhile keep the door of your mansion
unlocked and your whereabouts a mystery.
And if you will write poetry, then
observe the disciplines, attend to scansion.

(xiii) *Homage to Kyffin Williams*

When my mother met him last, in London,
at the Royal Academy, he shook
her hand and said, 'Thank you for that *Kyffin*.
They call me Kiffin here.' The look
of laughter in his eye. In Wales they say
you are what you speak. But that's hardly
all-inclusive of the national family.
Let's add for him: 'You are what you see.'

And what he sees is Wales and its *cynefin*,
marking the canvas of his heart with brisk
knife-work, from Menai shore to Llŷn,
man and boy, under Yr Wyddfa's moody gaze.
Stormlight in his quick look and instant risk
to rescue truth from time's high seas.

(xiv)

'Mc maybe I am…' not aptly ap. Nor
did my father know Lloyd George, but he knew
Saunders Lewis; and others too who
had 'walked Fron-goch', with Collins, for
the duration of those Troubles we were spared
…except that time the IRA exploded
a bomb at Kinmel Army Camp in Clwyd
(so Brendan had thought to blow up Cammell Laird)

…give or take a second home or two in Llŷn.
I'm no *Cymro*, no incendiarist either.
I live in middle England now, lost in
my middle years, found wanting too:
except that I know what I come from, and where,
bind me forever to my point of view.

(vii) *'Prophecy' from Iolo Goch's* Last Poems

If failure is all you have known, perhaps
you had far better learn to love it as
the blighted seed of promise that it was
than despair entirely? Survive on scraps.
And if the pathos of those near misses,
defeat snatched from the jaws of victory,
afford you solace, like the mystery
in poetry, then make good your losses.

Six hundred years is a long time to wait.
And what you waited for bears no likeness,
not the remotest resemblance, to what
has arrived, or he could begin to dream,
or you have forgotten. None the less,
you do well now to honour his name.

(viii) *9/18/1400*

That autumn morning, out of the wide blue
future, when they razed the town of Rhuthun
to ground zero, how many of them knew
what was afoot? Not even Owain.
Though he would prove as good a strategist
as any of them, from Odysseus
to Osama, from Allah back to Zeus,
the best laid schemes are only so much mist.

So I write here, now, like the lost remnant
of his retinue, or *plaid*, pursuing
lines of attack on the spur of the moment.
Deluded like most people that I know
enough to be doing what I'm doing
and why on earth I might be doing so.

(ix) *A Monoglot Trout*

First light, in England, travelling westward,
meets me looking for it, up for it at
scraich of innocence again, drop-of-a-hat:
a boy-man rising ten who clambered,
nervous at heart, to look time in the eye,
reticent in simple hope and silence
of loud wilderness: deliverance
that held me captive then, and will until I die.

When the bailiff came and said in English:
'I don't suppose you have a permit?'
Maredydd turned and offered him a fish.
I turned in silence and looked away.
So licence waived for a monoglot trout,
brithyll (in Welsh), we lived to fish another day.

(x)

When young Owain went to Bod Alaw,
the Welsh School in Colwyn (founded
in 1950), you'd think he was retarded,
and his parents thick. How could they allow
him to miss so much, fall behind forever,
in his rough flannel shorts, his pebble specs?
It made no sense. 'A language no one speaks,
except to the sheep and the weather.'

'Welsh-Welsh…' or 'thick Welsh', they'd say meaning both
twp and spluttering guttural Babel.
As to their poetry! It beggars belief
that it doesn't translate, they'd sneer. As if
they knew all about the art of the *Awdl*
and *Englyn*, and the rules of *Cynghannedd*.

(xi)

As if… But whatever became of him?
Was that his reflection I saw one night
in an estate agent's window? The light
poor, as I remember, and prospects dim.
Was that his handiwork at the roadside
declaring NID YW CYMRU AR WERTH
and SAESON ALLAN, for all he was worth?
Which was very little, set against his pride.

The beauty of it always was the way
he disappeared, or went to earth.
Either he's alive or he's dead, they'd say
at court à la Rumsfeld, the Prince of Wales
become the Prince of Annwfn and myth,
to prove how in truth repression fails.

(xii) *On the Study of Celtic Literature (1866)*

for Robert Young, after Tom Paulin

Didst not thou sow good seed in thy field?
From whence, then, hath it tares?
                                        Matthew xiii, 27

'The sooner the Welsh language disappears,'
said St Matthew Arnold, '…the better'
and he meant every word to the letter.
Though he rattles on about wheat and tares,
as if in the name of sweetness and light,
make no mistake: what governs the page
of this *bien-pensant* Victorian Sage
is imperialist sweetness and shite.

Meanwhile, back at the Eisteddfod,
as high above the Irish Sea he stood
pontificating about the need to drive
the 'English wedge' into the very Welsh
–Welsh heart of Wales, the natives strove
to judge the best essay on: 'What it means to be English'

(xv) *Ubi Sunt*

for Nicolas Jacobs

Just as those scholars at Oxford closed
their books and left their pens, to rally
to the cause, so, courtesy of Bodley,
I open mine and read and note bemused
to write a poem and trace them home.
But no key unlocks the time, or flight
on creaking air reveals their fate
down here below, to save them (and my poem).

What became of them? I don't find them
named in any memorial; though I still see
the look of one and hear the odd accent from,
say, Bethel, in Turl Street, now and then,
but fewer than ever there used to be.
What became of them? Where have they gone?

(xvi) *On Burning the British Library*

Where would we be without the old motifs?
What was, what might have been… the cross
to bear, wrongs to feed the flames of loss
and further faith in our beliefs?
But when men start to burn books? It's not
that they are cold and trying to get warm
but that they want to wipe you out…

At which poetry makes everything happen.
For things are not just as they seem,
and not just unjust, but beyond reason.
History's a smokescreen to a mystery.
And there's no smoke without a conflagration.
When Black Ysgolan torched the British library,
he lit a fire that forged a nation… literally.

(xvii) *The Irish Question*

The time word takes to travel is unreal:
rumour's rampant, youths and rascals rally,
rabbles rouse, run ragged, rout, horrify:
next thing you know it's out of control.
Until here's a party at another game,
pursuing by stealth the English cause:
for Shakespeare's timely motive was
to put an Irish wolfhound in the frame.

For Owain read O'Neill. A fuse I lit
by chance in number three and fizzing in
fourteen explodes beneath my feet.
For O'Neill read… They stole from their own.
I pillage Henry for a line, just to begin
again, again… until all cover's blown.

(xviii) *'Gwalia'*

after the Welsh: 'Cywydd' by Gerard Manley Hopkins

i.m. E. Meirion Roberts

There is a merry brightness here, gushing
streams from many fountains, rain and dew.
You'll hardly find a country of such hue
in orbit anywhere, such rushing
succulence. Here thrust of water will
bring faithful witness (man will not),
to our valley's immortal look and lot
and only man's deficiency work ill.

Here as from the hand of god see spring
beauty of true goodness, and nourishment
of faith, pure healing bring.
Who'd disagree with that? Or with his last
wish or will and testament
deny the holy grandchildren he blessed?

(xix) Inferno: *The Superhighway*

So tell me whose brutish prophecy
was it we saw fulfilled in the North
that time, when, between the Dragon and his wrath,
they gouged the coast for the Expressway?
Expressly it seemed to drain life from
the country. A rat-run not a by-pass
built to turn the land- and sea-scape to a mess.
As if to say, all roads lead to Rome.

Who could ask for anything more?
So Gerard, now, god bless the holy
grandchildren, drugged up *ar lan y môr.*
Long live the urban wilderness yet,
our hearts in hiding from our folly.
But at least, be praised, the rain's still wet.

(xx) Purgatorio: *The Long March*

That morning we got in under the hag
overhang below Clogwyn, a sheep-shelter
tagged with wool, and took stock, huddled there,
as the rain drove home its attack, over bog
and rock and wilderness of Wales below,
the day still young and we already
miles on our way, a raggle-taggle army
of foot, with more than the worst to go.

Owain, Maredudd, the old man, and me:
a mere boy in their company, voiceless;
on that cold, wet, mean March march to try
our luck up there (with a March Brown?),
but even they got cold feet (god bless!)
and began to weigh up the march down.

(xxi) Paradiso: *Dulyn, 1957*

It was discipline and fleetness of mind
and footwork in the old metres carried
the day up there, those days bedazzled
by sun and cloud running on the wind.
The poets prolific in all they touched,
quick to hook their lines into the rising
poems, whether at dawn, midday or evening.
They could do nothing wrong. And it seemed

Wales was theirs forever, rain or shine.
No one came up that far but if he did
they knew him without looking twice,
come over the top from nearer heaven
and shared a brew and said, word of god,
they'd find no better day in Paradise.

(xxii) *Wake for Owain*

There is no end where there's a beginning.
Searching for the way ahead, if not,
as seems impossible, the exit,
I'm driving down the motorway, wondering
where I'll find him next, and listen as I go
to Patrick Healy's *Finnegans Wake*
(on 17 CDs) to check (for pity's sake)
did Shem the Punmanmawr en route to
Holyhead (longest way round, shortest home),
in douce dŵr anywhere harbour Owain?
This day wet as Bethesda now, I come
looking to park. Little I dream he'll surface.
Until, like Tom Tim Tarpey the Welshman,
by chance sails by: GLENDOWER PLACE.

(xxiii) *For Diana, i.m. Mrs Glyn Dŵr*

Don't wake up for me dear: I'm only
nextdoor in my study, burning
the midnight oil; or can you hear me singing?
Far worse to have been his wife, lonely
all year those years, and in the morning.
Don't fret to feel me rise early,
at least you know where I am, only
a thin partition away, at my calling.

One thing more seems likely to be true:
I'll survive my enemies' worst scorn, and when
they're done, they'll hardly come for you.
I would ask what was it like for her
to be caught up in history? But then
she wasn't, much, was she? Not so you'd hear.

(xxiv)

Suppose it had worked out? The sonnets
constellated like points of light about
a laurel crown, not spiked by my thorny heart.
But all I can say is: 'I had my moments…':
brief alliances of sound and sense; old
loyalties; love for which there is no choice;
the native tenor of my singing voice;
unlooked for ways, as poems unfold:

quick progress day by day, and slower
week by week, a task, as the proverb says
like fetching water over a river.
So Glyn Dŵr toiled in that sequence of events
and came no closer but to end his days
saying thornily, 'I had my moments'?

37

(xxv) *Y Werin*

And the rest... the atrocities of war:
for tares read depleted uranium.
And for wool, the trade in opium:
those ancient local staples of the poor,
who always pay the price of others' pride,
as interest on their own. Time out of mind
is theirs. Their principality to find,
when armies clash, there is no place to hide.

But they're the first, *y werin,* to be true,
first and last, always there, at the wall,
witness to whatever men like Owain do.
In time they'll tell you how the die was cast
and show what was the future after all,
and not the last convulsions of the past?

(xxvi) *Aubade*

You chose to begin? Well, not exactly.
You chose to go on? I wouldn't say so.
You believed in it? As far as I know.
You understood your aim? Imperfectly.
There were things I thought I might say,
and I waited up for them to occur.
Others I laboured to discover,
came overnight, with the light of day.

Like the Emerald Isle Express, rattling
along, as I dug for bait by Conwy;
or out on Colwyn shore, unhooked whiting,
gwyniad, from a nightline. High hopes then
no less at the mercy of luck. If mercy
it is, or luck that longing to begin.

(xxvii) *The Emerald Isle Express*

I knew where you came from before I knew
your destination: see destiny and
nation pun, as if they understand
how poems and railways work. My dreams grew
a network from the moment I looked up,
at your seashore mirrors, shimmying off,
with allure of elsewheres, and promise of
escape, to worlds not on my little map.

They went in droves. The depredation such
as left no choice, English-Made-Easy in
their pockets, and the rough guide to getting rich.
Then travelled to and fro, like Thomas with Yeats;
O'Donoghue his 'rainmaker' at Colwyn;
on that fine line between nation and mental states.

(xxviii) *Epilogue*

If it was worth fighting for it was
worth losing. That has to be the logic.
There's no true life but risks the tragic,
on whatever scale. But now the danger is:
victors' 'justice', the State's high hand,
chorused by the *Telegraph* and *Sun*.
Meanwhile, Owain limped on the run,
his language his true shield, his hope and
faith, to hide and comfort him. Through the valley
of the shadow of death he crept, by thicket
and cave, his consolation not to die
betrayed. Until the day dawned he found
(no one knows where), that little wicket
gate to Annwfn, where he was crowned.

May my poor tribute touch: the sorrow
in your heart, that drove you to enlist;
the guilt and grief you carried in your breast,
its aftertaste foretasted, in all you saw
and wrote of mortal loss, and waste,
between the eye and the object; joy,
that queer word gay, as when a wide-eyed boy
you first stepped out, a latecomer at last,
on the wild road, foot soldier herald
to the birds and broken ranks of hedge.
Life's storm and war's storm since still sharpen their music,
in deadly earnest. But you stand on here and hold
the ground for us, forever, on the stark page,
singing like a thrush, to cut us to the quick.

Homage to Patagonia

Do you not see that the world is done.
'Lament for Llywelyn, The Last Prince', d. 1282, Gruffudd ab yr Ynad Coch

(i) *Mysterious Are the Ways of God*

Rain fell in the mountains,
at Nebo it rained all day.
From Bethel to Bethesda, on
all those Biblical names,
the rain fell, world without end.
It rained in Welsh *bwrw glaw*.

It rained even harder in English.
And there was consternation
and gnashing of teeth.
And the preacher preached
of the children of Israel's
likeness to the children of Wales.

(While in mid-Patagonia the climate,
his 'Handbook' rough guide said,
was: 'very pleasant and adaptable
to the Welshman's constitution',
with 142 rainy days to 158 in Wales
and the heavens burst as he read.)

And it rained and the hills bucked
and kicked as the clouds galloped by.
In an unlettered world the Word
leapt from the page. (Some things
must be believed to be seen.)
Mysterious are the ways of God.

So every Sunday Calvin said.
And the valleys swarmed
but not with the honey-bee,
and the hills emptied and filled.
And Bessemer-Bessemer
hissed the iron like a serpent.

Rail upon rail the future called,
all aboard, all aboard,
the Patagonian Express. *Chu
-but, chubut...* Borges was appalled.
But the people boarded nonetheless:
one-way to the ends of the earth.

(ii) *Witness Lost Souls*

At the very ends of the mind… and what
held me there, barely sane, as now must seem
to anyone at such a distance from
my doom, bidding goodbye to all that.
But grant me please at least the latitude
you'd grant yourself. And longitude?
To one who longing went as if pursued
into the wilderness and solitude.

And what on earth was that about? Unlike poles
attract, like poles repel, I understand.
Extremes meet. As witness lost souls
ad infinitum who cross wild seas
and change their skies to comprehend
integrity and faith as truth decrees.

(iii) *Against the Afflictions of the Taskmasters*

I wander out onto this page to find
grey wilderness of thorns, loud with Hudson's observations,
before him Darwin's; and Fitzroy's
narratives ramped up in the 'Handbook'
like the History of Moses,
who'd never see the promised land.

One found his faith at last just as
the other found it falsely grounded.
So truth will out. By natural selection?
They passed like ships in the night,
yet both aboard the *Beagle* bound
south to Port Desire.

And it snowed butterflies as far as the eye could see,
until light and water melted with them…
So once upon the deep I saw
poems swarm about the ocean too
in starry-eyed and phosphorescent air
that crooked flight I made to Inis Mór.

No sooner Genesis than hard on its heels
it's time to leave. I AM WHO AM, I
AM hath sent me unto you.
I punned and fooled. (I thought it best
to be up and go. The heart of standing is
you cannot fly, crooked or otherwise.)

That butterfly in the wilderness: *c'est moi*, who AM *iambic*
against the afflictions of the taskmasters
and cast a flutter shadow on this page to say
this is my name for ever and this
is my memorial, evolve or die? But
how odd of God to choose the Welsh?

As witness here their Exodus,
to save the language and preserve
their heritage and true religion,
in the backside of the desert, at the ends of the earth
where only the fittest or least fit
for this world survive.

44

(iv) *Several Families Came from the Slate-Quarrying Areas*
of North Wales...

The more you read the more you wonder...
Rain-without-end from a sky of slate,
labour exploited... a repressive English State:
but all that way to change the weather?
They saw the light, as pristine as it foamed
in Magellan's wake, in phosphorous seas
that glowed pale light, and felt at ease
and all their grief the bracing air consumed.

So good so far. So far so good. And better far
to travel hopefully... (with: 300 sacks
of wheat, 800 sheep, 6 pigs, et cetera
a medical man to keep them alive;
three ministers to preach the chosen texts)
and better far (O God!) than to arrive.

(v) *The Thomases at San Tomis*

Between escaping from and escaping to:
the line's a fine one, always, as mad as any
poet's thin partition, as Ovid knew
with his one-way ticket: but he
at least wanted to return, to his beloved city.

While these in dreams of milk and honey
preferred to render unto Caesar
what was his. Though even they were surely
torn by doubt as the *Mimosa*
left port, and the world fell away under her…

Last nights and first make extremes meet
and box the compass of emotion.
But now at last they found their feet
upon the arid plain; beside the wheeling ocean
stood, confronted by their vision.

(vi) *In Toil and Love*

By the end of 1865 there was considerable doubt among the settlers as to whether or not they could survive the ensuing months. Glyn Williams

What plain comrades, my sisters and brothers,
honest as the day was long and arduous,
treking down the Chubut, speaking neither
of the master languages, your tongue
innocent as rain and your eyes like your hearts
wide open in pursuit of the dream.

It was like Book 1 in Virgil's *Georgics*
but everything was upside down: August
was winter with the fangs of Antarctica,
gnawing at the door, and snowfall sudden
– whiteness and the sea white as Melville's whale,
would take the breath away.

Lessons in husbandry all to be learnt
from scratch, scratch of plough in
abandoned meanders by the Chubut.
And the Chubut herself wild in her antics
and unpredictable the day,
the signs, the constellations unprecedented.

But error and judgement are man and wife
(not necessarily in that order) and
first one teaches then the other
and the lesson is habitual and pliant,
like those willow trees from which you took your bearings,
and what else is unspoken in toil and love

in modesty of faith and purpose. What else
but wonder at you now and praise
your resolution, your honest designs
on nothing but the better way,
as the Rio rose up out of the Old Testament
and washed your wheat into the sea.

(vii) *Dream-Bird*

So in the grain of all success rusts the seed of ruin.
Generations are as dust. Languages no less.
Though love however lost survive, no absolute
outlasts, though heart's unbroken,
and the poem retains its poetry, now here
now there, as light falls through the ages.

So Hudson waded ashore from shipwreck,
the nameless dream-bird of childhood
on the pampas pampered,
singing the song of itself in his head. A
dowdy bird but not a dowdy song,
its life short but its note mellifluous and long.

They got on well with the indigenous Tehuelche:
to whom their plainness, plainness of Y Werin
(hold at heart and carry to the grave), spoke
the minority languages known as human
and fair trade. Not Bible-tongue wherein
the lesson: to fear hostility of other tribes.

Yet it was on 'Israel in the Wilderness'
the minister preached his first sermon.
And, give or take an Eldorado quest (O calf of gold),
the text and testament that held them in duress
(little within great) remained the Old,
master narrative of the Hebrew scribes…

By the time it rose on thermals to the Andes
it was as nothing. But they kept their act together,
and took it as prescribed: attendant Pharisees,
vipers in their midst, on hand to round
the story out; snakes with human countenance,
marked with a cross, ugly (as Darwin found).

That serpent! How he insinuates. Spanish
of the Argentine lisping at the door,
and Satan in the body of a British engineer:
boorish imperialist A. P. Bell, surveyor
for the railway, whose hatred of the Welsh
matched his contempt for the native poor.

So Modernity would hunt by rail, and kill at the railhead,
the journey always one-way:
cattle-trucks crammed with living dead…
And the Tuhuelche foresaw and spoke the text,
once more of Paradise, and where it lay,
beneath the high sierra to the west…

I was born there… in Clwyd, I mean: nearest
likeness they could give the pleasant vale,
rich in berries and currants of every kind
with water-cress in gentle rivulets… And here they made
heaven-on-earth, and knelt, and prayed.
And all was as the good Lord said, in the timeless tale.

God save your poem from ruin.
Life divides to conquer and sub-divides
until we downsize to the clay-house,
the house of fire. Morbidity I don't rate
but courage to outstare it all.

As was yours, dying as you understood.
The poem can wait until it can't wait.
My shelves bow too with favourite books:
Ovid's *Tristia*, Fallon's *Georgics* now,
Walden, The Purple Land... and yours.

To which I add your anonymous friend's
Canto on the Last Flooding of the Chubut,
privately printed in Trelaw. In the belief
that those of us who dare to let the poem wait
earn our almonds and *apéritifs.*

(x) *Qué Lindo Dia!*

in homage to Hugh MacDiarmid

But this isn't a poem that prefers
the closed comfort of the Pullman...
or hankers for the theatres and cafés
of Buenos Aires,
scandal and gossip of the concourse.

This is an art or craft
should never care for that:
...voraciousness and sterility
of ignorance,
ambition and ingratitude.

But for the folk on whom the Bear
looks down in sleep
who dreamt their future into being
however briefly,
against the tyranny of fact.

Not change or travel but both
and forever, they knew
and did not know:
Mrs Davies' son unmarried yet
and God's promise to Cymru

vain? They won while they could
enough to prove
Qué linda familia!
Qué lindo dia!
in whatever tongue, as in their own.

(xi) *Songline for Kyffin*

in memoriam, annus mirabilis 1968–1969

O my dear friend may
god bless you I pray.

In that year we both
took to the ends of the earth.

And reached beyond reason
the same conclusion.

In Memoriam Dylan Thomas (1914–1953)

However it was your poems flew in
-to my head, they left me spellbound:
slow to wake and see, for the sound
of an alphabet's heavenly din.
Better late than never hides a multitude
of sins; belatedness, the *cause célèbre*
of every kind of imperious failure,
may still possess a poignant pulchritude.

The ashes I rake are the sands of time
disappearing through my fingers.
Roused by the rub of grain and rhyme,
I stand up to hymn your praises, even now,
down all my nearer sixty summers,
on this my heart's raised hearth, down here below.

This is a companion piece for sure,
for here we toil and share our labour
like the original pair, no moping or lusting
after lost youth, but what adds up
to agape's absorption from the world.

If the snake oil salesman should call
we'll not hear him out here, no matter
our plot's so small, we can hardly
lose sight of each other even with
our backs turned, as we reach or kneel

to bud or bed, trimming and snipping
and digging, talking intermittently,
pragmatically, apropos of whatever it was
should go where, and the garden blesses us
with its classic thought and shade.

Virtuous purpose has great merit,
for it can banish desire for solitude
and yet provide escape from company...
Which is the better way to be? To ask
a question of a mystery? Or answer with one?

We work the soil here so diligently
anything might grow in its season. I say,
I can't decide in which mood I'm happier.
You think I prefer an edge of satire,
some bittersweet version of pastoral?

I certainly like to prune the apple.
But best of all, I like the fall, slapstick,
as the first cold snap signals the game is up
and gravity grasps the nettle itself
to bring everything down to earth.

Dog Days

September has been sending out
subversives, in behind August's lines.
At first I thought it was the grain
ripening, clicking open in
summer glower, but it was rain.

Then barrage of gales and deluge
to soften up the country,
dashing my hopes to harvest early
and holiday away from here
somewhere happy with you.

No matter ink holds leaf to branch
and stubbornly the heart weathers.
Expeditionary forces
return from the hill, half-drowned.
I copy out my verses.

And see them scout ahead
Indian file, on the *qui vive*.
Nothing changes they say
unless you can imagine it.
Not every dog has his day.

So winter was the devil's work?
At any rate, it drives us from the garden in
to gaze at wet and cold; drab northern dearth,
but for moments of heartening
focus, bare trees and aftermath.

The sudden blackbird metamorphosed
to pin and brooch, to broach and pin
the worm, stares; and we stare
into it: the soul's gaze engaged
in metaphysics, root and branch?

I swear next year we won't
make the same mistakes again:
as if there aren't others out there,
just waiting to befall us, infinite
opportunities for error in

our haven from the world's chaos.
You say, if only I would read instructions.
What is the male imagination for?
For Eve the tree of knowledge,
the seedsman's packet?

For Adam the bungled metaphor?
Imperfection makes the world go round…
Practice makes perfect observation
not perfection… Nothing finite can
determine its own being…

So I protest too much my incompetence
and folly. Life cannot end well,
I fear, and all's not for the best.
But study harder how
to cultivate your garden, none the less.

Poem

The day's rain swells the river,
the spate bigger by the hour.

What foils the salmon leaping
is not, as I thought, too much water

but too little. So let it pour and pour!
Then what's not faith is timing.

Arkwork

The Loss of *The Princess Victoria*, January 1953

Abandon ship all you who enter here

(i) *Noah's Flood*

The known world, and the unknown, under water,
and by the mid-point, as one might suppose,
where things had got to heaven knows.
And had the scuppers failed in that foul weather
or had we struck a hidden rock there was
no other ground on which to run aground.
Then all was lost and no redeeming lost-and-found,
no memorial, come whatever time to pass…

A single window like an eye, reeling,
three tiers or decks but none to promenade
and take the air on, or watch the evening
sun go down, with a drink in one hand,
the other on the taff-rail. No headway made,
though the world go round, no good dry land.

(ii) *No Doubt*

But tell me what the mystery's about?
The price we pay to keep ourselves afloat
exacted by a metaphor, no doubt.
A boat, I cry, your kingdom for a boat.
For it's not mine, and nothing is: the air
I sing and breathe all begged or borrowed
as were those dreams I thought I followed,
a stowaway who can't afford the fare.

You know those times when you would rather not?
The weather's up and blusters at the door,
the rain is down your neck and in your boot:
on such a day did Noah's flood begin
but still you sail as if ordained by law.
Well, such a plight it is that I am in.

No good? No good? If land, not to be seen.
Kirk's on the hill but the hill's drowned
as the river rises up and round
and like Leviathan lays waste the scene.
Kirk itself's an ark on an uneven keel
but nothing of that old salvation ever
freed itself from violence: O brother,
for whom was hellfire and it was real.

Hell to pay for her owners none the less.
A nineteenth-century disaster in
the twentieth, his honour said. A slight breeze
in cat's paws crossed to the Causeway
as he spoke. The sea waltzed in and out again,
as it has always done, since Noah's day.

Two hours out on the interminable
waterways, he signalled she was no longer
'under command'. The wind blew stronger.
The sea rose and his ark unstable
rolled round the rolling world. Still nothing
in the offing told him where they were.
Pure storm, pure element of air
and water beaten to the eye, drowning.

Any port in a storm he bade the raven.
Anywhere, he said, from Ararat to Osney,
not knowing how near she stood to haven
at the mouth of Belfast Lough. (God save us!)
But the day proved just one more – of how many? –
in the wilderness of hope and loss.

(v) *In Memory of David Broadfoot, Radio Officer*

O steadfast Captain Ferguson what doom
your ark, what fatal ferryman you proved...
Souls perish and hands go down. She waved
him off as usual, from the front bedroom,
and the house as empty as a widow
in the buffeting wintry shock of day.
This woman mother now so far away
of my wife's cousin's husband? Somehow
related, anyway... and how remote
that morning (many tumultuous lines
cross-hatch, scribble, lower the boat),
as David Broadfoot gave his life,
sinking fast... radioing lifelines
to the last, and, choking, came to grief.

(vi) *May-Day*

A single window like an eye and morse
remorselessly… remorseful. Always when
the drama is in progress, another one
is going on behind the scenes, and worse
remembrance runs and runs like the mousetrap,
a play within and another one beyond.
So that was Rosencrantz, packet to hand,
and Guildenstern, blithely taking a nap.

Had they the serum to hand in Eden
would any of this have fallen out?
Noah went to the bridge: Leviathan
wrapped him round and round his heart,
saying: 'It's all in the telling, whether heaven
or hell, and all in the name of art.'

They went aboard in ones and twos,
in no great shape or order. The usual
kind of crowd and would be casual
but for those quayside feeling queasy blues.
They were thrown together... (Excuse me.)
But they'd need more than dry Ulster humour
to keep their spirits above water,
as they gasped and struggled in the sea.

Meanwhile, deep inland, the steading hove to.
As if a poem on the shipping forecast
was that moment conceiving. The radio
announced the disaster, in patrician English:
the old assault and innocence lost
that poetry is heir to, and the Irish.

(viii) *A Cowshed High Up In the Alps*

In the mountains, there you feel free.
T.S. Eliot

Is it really that we want to be free
of memory's dirty tricks? Without which
there's no idealism, no utopia, and not much
else to speak of; and the cowshed you see
high up in the Alps, an upended ark,
is a cowshed. But if we could strip it
of association what might it not
be said to be? Shelter, hafod, womb-dark?
None of the above. That way madness lies.
So Gudrun can only stand and watch
as Gerald wanders off into the snow and dies.
I lived in an ark once, all run aground
upon the rocks. I can see it from here, which
believe me is the better way round.

(ix) *Noah: The Complete Works*

He might have landed on Mont Blanc.
He might have grounded on Parnassus.
He might have drifted by Ben Nevis.
He might have struck a rock and sunk.
He might have voyaged up the Congo.
He might have cruised above the Nile.
He might yet round the Horn in style...
He might have travelled incognito
and told another kind of shipwreck tale.
He might have written *Robinson Crusoe*
or the one about the great white whale.
He might have shot the poor albatross
like cock robin with his bow and arrow...
And had he not how could we count the loss?

(x) *Art Lubber*

Keep your feet on the ground that's how.
Those 133 lives lost know no accounting or
grieving now. Just nine poems out before
she sprang a leak below the bow,
as if she'd struck the Whillans of Larne.
Like young Morrison all out of luck,
he foundered on a heartfelt rock
and could neither sail on nor return.

Cut your losses and swim for it. Think of it
in metres and work to improve your style,
and do what you will with the lifeboat it
can be to no avail, either to the dead
or the living, if you haven't learnt to sail,
in the name of art, as the monster said.

(xi) *Covenant*

In my heart's wake a catalogue of wrecks,
drownings: from *Deutschland* to *Eurydice*,
from 'Lycidas' to the 'Cast-Away', the
Mariner's guilt, the spectral decks,
a slave-ship hulk, old Ahab's curse...
creation myths; survival stories
recounted by Ulysses *in extremis*.
The sea has many voices. And nothing worse

happens but happens there, unless in verse?
Ten sheets to the wind and half seas over
and I could to my own self be true (what else?),
I'd go down again with the good ship Elegy
on a dog-toothed covenant wing-and-prayer
to see all the world as it flashed before me.

North Clutag

(i) *A Poacher's Handbook*

My undercover name
north-north-west indeed
of where I make my home
down here among the dead.

I was found in a dark wood:
last light, running at its edge
(filigree, wood-cut), stood
caught in a thorny hedge.

The page beneath my hand,
now foxed, gave all it had to give.
But my heart was green and
wanted what it couldn't have.

Light and air, North by your leave…
Sprigged lettering hedged about
with too much to grieve
for and too much to leave out.

(ii) *clutarche*

(1594–7 spelling)

Don't look back? What else to do?
Having put your hand to the poem
fit yourself for the kingdom of earth.

And as you reap, so shall you sow.
You have no say in any scheme.
Do what you will to keep the faith.

(iii) *Andy Walker (Ploughman)*

Not him but his father
who went for a soldier

and disappeared: lost in the action
of that wild fiction.

One of the fallen unsung
resurrected in his son

who followed the plough again
as this one follows the pen.

A stone cut with 'a waved top'
shows how the waters rose up.
They buried the martyrs there,
on Wigtown hill, above the river
where they drowned, and never
a dry eye in the house. And never
would Margaret 'hear' or 'swear'
but kept her covenant forever,
as the sea rose again, like Christ
Himself, but with a salty taste,
until the drowning light was past
and all the world in brutal haste
went about its business to the last,
trailing clouds of savage light
to feed the lie and keep it bright.

(v) *Covenant*

Whenever came a time to raise a glass
and toast: 'God save the King!'
he'd say beneath his breath, for all to hear:

'If He pleases... if He pleases...'
As if he was John Knox, not merely
your parish blacksmith John McNeillie.

(vi) *The Carry*

(Pronounced 'kerry')

There were days he said it changed
several times an hour, the skies confused.

Whether as night fell, or in the morning,
and what might come, come without warning.

Fair days or foul, a good practical Scot
he proved, and master of his craft.

At furnace and anvil forged shoe or share
or tinkered some ingenious repair

to keep the harvest running, one step ahead
of the weather, in whose cup he read.

Fay as they come, fay as any *spalpín* Irishman,
or foolish poet, with all his loss to scan.

(vii) *For Great-Granny Elizabeth*

(née *McGarva*)

Here I am then at your door,
late windfall of life's storm.

A man who'll tinker at a poem
until the kye come home.

For 'a wee bit hot water'
Mistress if you please.

Slower

Slower, the sign said, gently, inviting reflection,
expressing welcome, down the single-track way
through the grove, not an injunction. So we wove,
slower, through the rain, headlights strobing where
blonde sponge-like Charolais gazed at us, balefully,
drenched together under an oak. Only in Ireland
somebody said, too readily. But slower, the word itself
weighed in me all week, an undertow to all we did
and all we saw and heard during our stay,
on the banks of the Swilly at Castle Grove. Derry
just down the road, and farther east 'the real loo-loos',
as a guest from Wicklow said, up to no good.

Slower, the day called, rooks funnelling up through
pristine aftermath and down to dewy meadows where
the river slithered out over itself. Mrs Sweeney, a name
to conjure with, told us the history of the house. How
when the line of Groves died out, a niece of Queen
Elizabeth acquired it, but when Lord Mountbatten
got blown up she opted out. (Sotheby valued the contents
at over a million.) So the dairy-farming Sweeneys
seized the hour and moved in; and slower they thought,
slower they said, naming the rooms after Irish writers:
Swift, Wilde, Joyce, Yeats… as if to inspire
a happy addition to the literature of the Irish hotel.

Slower, they all said, but one told me how the Irish Army
had haunted his fields after Bloody Sunday and
the talk was of invasion, to liberate occupied territory
from the bloody Brits. Another said the 'Bs' hadn't
been all bad. You knew where you were with them.
But talk as they might, in sixty-eight no one saw it coming.
He'd been sent as a boy to school in Derry and when
the women of the Bogside chased the peelers out
with broom-handles, the boys thought it a great joke.
And so together we juggled terms and jinked down
unmarked borders of speech, like smugglers, refusing
to pay duty on our goodwill, shadowed by Good Friday.

Slower, history beckoned, sifting its river-silts so
late in the day, yet in the long run, as the man said,
in the long run we are all dead. And one said you know
if they had a referendum in England it would be for
a United Ireland. They want this over. But slower
our eyes said, slower, as we wearied of our troubles
and went upstairs to bed. Slower, we sank down,
out of our depth and beyond help, returned to our
failings and powerless privacies, our commonplace
desires: the bride and groom flown, and the wedding
of two worlds behind us. Maybe in their lifetime? Or
slower yet, their children's? Or their children's?

Quicker (Go Little Book)

Quicker? I agree. That was the word
I was looking for. Quicker to move on.
Quicker to say: 'Good-bye to all that.'

Quicker than you can say knife.
Quicker cut yourself free. Quicker than
the dead ever did. Quicker, I agree.

Notes

Glyn Dŵr Sonnets

For Owain Glyn Dŵr (c.1354–c.1416) read R.R. Davies's classic *The Revolt of Owain Glyn Dŵr* (OUP, 1995, 1997). The epigraph is from the legendary 'History of the Kings of Britain' (*Historia Regum Britanniae*) by Geoffrey of Monmouth, completed in 1136 (Penguin, 1966).

(i) For Shakespeare's portrayal of 'Glendower' see *I Henry IV*; and for Captain Fluellen, a foundational Welsh stereotype, see the more pervasively influential *Henry V.*

(ii) Pumlumon or its vicinity was the scene of a lightning guerrilla victory by Glyn Dŵr's forces. Lewis Valentine (1893–1986), minister and writer (whose brother Stanley was our next-door neighbour), with the writers Saunders Lewis (1893–1985) and D.J. Williams (1885–1970), served nine months in Wormwood Scrubs for setting fire in 1936 to building materials at an RAF bombing school at Penyberth in Llŷn. The local jest was that, on reaching the site at Penyberth, the idealistic would-be arsonists discovered they'd forgotten the matches and had to go back for them.

(iii) De Valera's extraordinary visit to Caernarfon, arranged by the local branch of the NUT, was reported in the *North Wales Weekly News,* 2 February 1950. It was a gesture of solidarity that Glyn Dŵr might have envied, given Irish reluctance seriously to commit to the support of his cause. 'Cymru am byth' = Wales for ever (ironically: 'byth' derives from an Irish loanword).

(iv) For 'cynefin', see sonnet v.

(vi) The prophetic tradition was very much alive in medieval Welsh culture and significantly informed Glyn Dŵr's view of the world. For Merlin's prophecies see Geoffrey of Monmouth (cited above). Hopcyn ap Tomas ab Einion (c.1330–*post* 1403), scholar and patron of poets, oversaw compilation of *Llyfr Coch Hergest* ('The Red Book of Hergest'), perhaps the most important of all the Welsh manuscript collections (owned by Jesus College, Oxford). In it are transcribed the prophecies of Merlin on which Hopcyn was an acknowledged authority. Glyn Dŵr consulted Hopcyn for his interpretation of them in 1403.

(vii) The poet Iolo Goch (c.1325–c.1398) is best known for his poem celebrating 'The Court of Owain Glyndŵr at Sycharth'. He died before the rising. The present poem from the apocryphal posthumous collection, *Last Poems*, draws presciently on the prophetic tradition.

(viii) Glyn Dŵr was proclaimed Prince of Wales at Glyndyfrdwy on 16 September 1400, and in his initial campaign, 18–23 September, he razed Rhuthun to the ground and devastated other towns in north-east Wales.

(ix) 'scraich' as in 'scraich of day' is a Scots word for the very first suggestion of dawn.

(x) Complex metrical rules and intricate rhyme-schemes render traditional Welsh poetry about as untranslatable and inimitable as poetry gets, even at the hands of the most ingenious practitioners, such as, for example, W.H. Auden.

(xi) NID YW CYMRU AR WERTH = Wales is not for sale; SAESON ALLAN = English out. 'Annwfn' (or 'Annwn') is the name for the Celtic 'Otherworld', a place of great well-being, located either on an island or under ground (see no. xxi below). Donald Rumsfeld: blunt and bellicose henchman of the George W. Bush regime.

(xii) In the opening to his book we find Matthew Arnold at Llandudno, whither he has gone to observe the natives at their Eisteddfod. The proceedings were of course conducted in Welsh, not a language with which Arnold was conversant.

(xiii) In some respects, Kyffin Williams (1918–) is to post-Second World War Welsh painting what his friend R.S. Thomas was to its poetry. But he has greater empathy with country and people and lacks the latter's religious angst. The last line of this poem alludes to Williams's descent from pioneering and heroic lifeboatmen on Ynys Môn.

(xiv) Fron-goch is a village near Bala where in 1889 Price of Rhiwlas attempted to establish a whisky distillery. The buildings of this failed venture were used after 1916 to intern Irish Republicans, including Michael Collins. The incident at Kinmel Camp, the stark shock of which to a child I will never forget, occurred in the mid-1950s. Brendan Behan (1923–1964)'s designs on the Cammell Laird Shipyard at Birkenhead were forestalled by his arrest in Liverpool in 1939.

(xv) *Ubi Sunt*: a motif fashionable in medieval poetry in Latin, meaning: 'Where are…'. Jesus College, or Coleg Iesu, is or was until recently, pre-eminently the Welsh college in the University of Oxford.

(xvi) The legend of infamous 'Black' Ysgolan and the burning of British books surfaces across a considerable span of Welsh (and Breton) history, from the twelfth century to the Glyn Dŵr rebellion, and beyond. He is said to have set fire to books accumulated by members of the Welsh nobility imprisoned in the Tower of London by Edward I, and so to have destroyed a vital tradition of writing and record, including the original Bible in Welsh. What escaped his attentions then, he returned to consume during the rebel-

91

lion, as a figure of English vengeance. See Philip Schwyzer's fascinating book *Literature, Nationalism and Memory in Early Modern England and Wales* (CUP, 2004).

(**xvii**) Shakespeare's *I Henry 1V* was first printed in 1598. In that decade (of the Nine Years War) it was the Gaelic Ulster Lord Hugh O'Neill (c.1550–1616) and Ireland proved troubling to the English State. As a guerrilla fighter O'Neill had not a fraction of Glyn Dŵr's genius; nor as a man, as Earl of Tyrone, bending his knee in the court of King James, in 1603, did he have Glyn Dŵr's resolve and integrity of spirit.

(**xviii**) For Gerard Manley Hopkins's 'Cywydd' see no. 172 in *The Poems of Gerard Manley Hopkins. Fourth Edition. Revised and Enlarged* (OUP, 1967). My version deliberately silences some of the religious features of the original to which I can't accommodate. It draws on a literal prose translation of the whole poem by my late friend E. Meirion Roberts (1913–1995), bard, illustrator and book designer. For 'heart in hiding' see Hopkins no. 36, 'The Windhover'.

(**xix**) 'ar lan y môr': 'by the seashore'. 'Come not between the dragon and his wrath', Shakespeare, *King Lear* I.i.124.

(**xx**) Clogwyn-yr-eryr (Eagle Crag) at the eastern end of Cefn Tal-llyn-Eigiau (the high ridge above Eigiau lake), in north-eastern Snowdonia. 'March Brown', one of the best all-round trout flies, with mottled wings, yellow and brown body, and long tails.

(**xxi**) Dulyn (black lake) lies three hours by foot from the bottom of the Conwy valley, below the 600ft precipices of Craig-y-Dulyn, between Y Foel Fras and Carnedd Llywelyn. It was recorded in the seventeenth century, and so probably thrived much earlier in the oral culture, that if you watched by the lake on a 'spirit night' (All Hallows' Eve, May Day Eve, and Midsummer Eve) you would see those doomed to die in the year ahead. All we saw were sheep, trout and birdlife, and the shepherd from Llanfairfechan (who always lived to tell the tale).

(**xxii**) Patrick Healy's virtuoso reading of James Joyce's *Finnegans Wake* (1939), in 17 CDs, is available from Rennicks Auriton Publishing, 40 Bow Lane East, Dublin 2. For Tom Tim Tarpey see *Finnegans Wake*, p. 390. For Glendower Place, see the Old Brompton Road, South Kensington.

(**xxv**) Y werin: gwerin, meaning 'the folk, the people of Wales': for whom Owain has always enjoyed unconditional heroic status, as figured, for example, in the name Meibion Glyn Dŵr (Sons of Glyn Dŵr) adopted by activists in the 1980s, and now in an issue of postage stamps.

(**xxvii**) 'The Emerald Isle Express' was a boat train on the Holyhead–London LMS line; sometimes in the early morning, as I seem to recall, it